Pro Tips on How to Publish Yourself

CHARLES ST. ANTHONY
(Charles Ayres)

Copyright 2022

Images and Text owned by I.G. Studios LLC

THE CONTENTS

SET YOURSELF A LIMIT

You've got a book you want to write. Maybe you even have a series of books. You may have been trying to publish your work traditionally and have been experiencing difficulty getting the attention of the gatekeepers of the traditional publishing world.

Fear not, my publishing protégé. I believe everyone has a voice and that every voice is valid. Just because you can't get your book project out traditionally doesn't mean it shouldn't be out there for people to enjoy. Someone somewhere is eager to learn from your experience, and with current technology, self-publishing is easier than ever. Take control of your publishing destiny! Become your own publishing house.

In this short guide, I offer some insight into how to publish your own books as eBook, paperback, and audiobook. I've learned a great deal over the last ten years I've been self-publishing, and I wish to bestow my knowledge upon you. I hope you can avoid the mistakes I made and get your book out there.

The first question I pose to you is: "How long do you want to commit to this project?" I am an advocate of a strategy I call the "**Set Yourself a Time Limit**" philosophy i.e. say you'll try to get publishers to pick up your book within one or two years. If you don't succeed in getting a publisher during the set time limit, then go ahead and self-publish.

I give a time frame of one to two years because most book agents and publishers receive thousands of submissions from aspiring authors. It usually takes several months to reply—if they reply at all! I know you are passionate about writing, and it's your dream to write a book. But you know who else wants a book? The Instagram Influencer with one million followers. And that guy you saw on TV with the Pulitzer Prize. I'm not saying it is impossible; however, you are competing with plenty of formidable adversaries.

You're a creative person. You probably have other projects you wish to work on and experiences you want to enjoy. Don't waste too much of your precious time since there are other things you wish to achieve.

I spent six years writing and trying to get my first humorous memoir *Impossibly Glamorous* published. Then I decided to self-publish because I knew that someone somewhere would enjoy it. It turned out I was right. I didn't immediately become rich. I didn't roll around in royalty money like Scrooge McDuck in his Money Bin. What did happen was:

- People all over the world read my work—even as far away as India and Japan.

- Having my story out in print proved therapeutic and improved my mental health.

- It gave me a way to connect with people I wouldn't have otherwise had the opportunity to interact with.

- Now I have 6 eBooks available on most major platforms and have gained an international following.

And… **I LEARNED HOW TO SELF-PUBLISH.** A skill I am going to teach you now in my brisk *Guide to Self-Publishing*. Let's get started on your first book.

Pro Tip! Don't be intimidated by the file names you'll come across. I included a glossary at the end of this book in case I'm overwhelming you with new abbreviations. While reading, you'll come across EPUB files. These are the type of files that take your book as you have it in Word or Google Docs and present the text via HTML—a basic coding language—so they are viewable in eBook readers such as an Amazon Kindle or a Barnes & Noble Nook. These files even make eBooks readable on your mobile phone or tablet device such as an iPad.

In ancient times (like 10 years ago), Amazon used a file type called MOBI, but Amazon has deprecated the MOBI file. The only types of files you need to concern yourself with are EPUB for eBook and "Print-Ready PDF" for your print edition. Don't worry, you don't need to learn HTML. There are hundreds of talented coders on Upwork and Fiverr that will produce a beautifully presented EPUB at a reasonable price. You could do the file conversion yourself, but I prefer to entrust my eBooks to professionals.

YOUR FIRST BOOK OUT IN 10 MINUTES

Alright, let's get your first book out. First, you need to sign up with a self-publishing platform. Sign up to publish on Kindle eBook readers. Amazon's eBooks still make up the majority of eBook sales worldwide, and you can publish on Kindle by signing up to KDP. KDP stands for "Kindle Direct Publishing."

I also use another platform called Draft2Digital to publish on multiple platforms at the same time. Draft2Digital will get you on a variety of eBook platforms such as Apple Books and Sony Kobo, but let's start with just Kindle. You can publish on Kindle from Draft2Digital as well, but I still publish my Kindle books directly through KDP since they provide some in-house advertising and marketing methods that you don't find on Draft2Digital. We'll get to advertising in a second, but let's get your first book out!

Hop onto the Kindle Direct Publishing website and sign up for an account. You'll need to input your legal name and bank information for tax purposes. Yes, Uncle Sam will be asking for his cut of your royalties. The good news is your expenses while writing your book ***might be*** deductible, but you'll want to ask a tax professional about whether or not it applies to your publishing expenses.

Next, leave KPD for a second and open up a new file in Google Docs, since it allows you to save as an EPUB. Apple Pages also allows you to save as EPUB. Google Docs is free with every Gmail account, and you can whip out your phone and write in Docs while getting an oil change or waiting at the doctor's office. You can be writing whenever you have a few minutes to spare. If you have never used Google Docs before, hit the Google Apps in your Gmail, then scroll down to find the Google Docs icon.

Click the Google Docs icon to open it up and execute the following steps:

1. Start a new file by pressing the rainbow "+" icon.

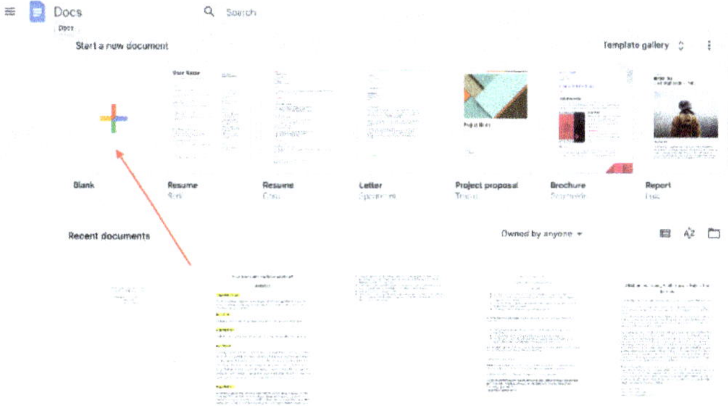

2. Write on the first page "This is my great book."

3. Under the File menu, download your sentence as an EPUB file.

4. Go back to KDP and press "Create" on the Bookshelf (home) screen. For purposes of this exercise, just say you are making an eBook.

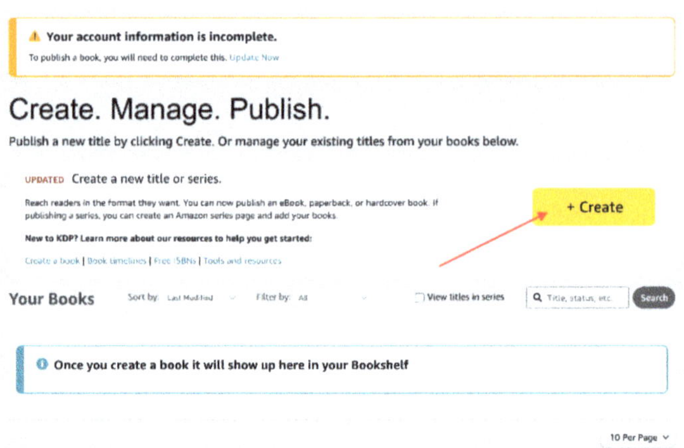

5. On the "Details" page, write your book title, author name, and blurb, and select the categories your book will fit into (romance, non-fiction, etc.)

6. Move onto the next screen in KDP, which is the "Content" page. Here you'll upload the Epub file you just created. You can make a free cover on the "Content" page too.

7. Move onto the "Pricing" page in KDP where you will set the price for your masterpiece worldwide.

8. In the lower right corner of the pricing page, **HIT PUBLISH!**

Voilà! You are now the author of one sentence! Bask in the glow of your success as an author.

I'm oversimplifying the whole thing, but if you boil self-publishing down to its basic parts, this is how simple the process is. Now we are going to apply this concept to the book you actually want to write. Creating written content that is engaging and attractive enough that people will buy and read does take more effort than what I laid out in this chapter, but now you see what the process entails.

Pro Tip! It's on the KDP "Content" page that you will be asked if you have your own ISBN or if you want one of

Amazon's free ISBNs. An ISBN is a number that identifies your book to different merchants, libraries, and publishers. You can buy ISBNs in bulk for 10 or 100 at a time, but ISBNs also tend to be a bit expensive. I use the free ISBN with my recent books—it comes down to how much money you want to spend and how much power you want to give to Amazon. **Self-publishing can end up being an endless money suck**, so I think it wise to find places where you can be frugal. ISBNs are the first things I skimp on. In my opinion, the ISBN system is a relic of the pre-digital age.

THE TENETS OF SELF-PUBLISHING

Did anyone ever say to you, "Never judge a book by its cover"? While I agree with this old maxim with regard to people, when it comes to books, I believe that people judge books by their covers all the time. In fact, I would speculate that you judged this very book before you acquired it, as well. People will decide whether or not they will give your book a chance in a split second. If a cover looks enticing and the book typography appears professional, then you have a better chance of capturing readers' attention.

Also, your book is not just competing with other books, it will be competing for people's attention with other types of content. There is so much content available nowadays that it is impossible to keep track of every-thing. Your book will compete for people's attention against streaming via Netflix, movies at an old-fash-ioned movie theater, and video games. You are also up against the never-ending parade of free user-gener-ated content on YouTube, social media, and every-where you turn. You have only a moment to convince people that your book is worth their time.

My advice is to spend a little money on giving your book a professional look and feel—which is easier than ever thanks to freelancers on Upwork and Fiverr. The catch is you should set yourself a budget. As I mentioned in the last chapter, self-publishing can turn into an endless money suck with people everywhere lining up to put their hands in your pockets and empty them out. Here are my **Tenets of Self-Publishing** which will help you put your book together without breaking your bank ac-count. The Tenets also includes general guidelines I fol-low for each book I release.

1. **Your book can be self-published, but your book shouldn't *look* self-published.**

   A lot of people have joined the self-publishing revolution. And guess what? A lot of the work they put out looks amateur or poorly designed. Not to say their stories aren't still valuable and relevant, but you might only have 5 seconds (if that!) to convince someone that your book is valuable enough for them to give it their time.

   It doesn't have to be expensive, but a few dollars well-spent on cover design and other parts of the book will go a long way in luring new readers and enticing them to purchase your book. You can spend hundreds if not thousands of dollars on cover design, typography, and other graphics. I say don't waste a ridiculous amount of money. If you see a designer you like on Upwork or Fiverr with an economical price, and good previous ratings, go ahead and try them.

2. I also work as a voice-over talent, and one of the main principles in that world is, "If it sounds

good, it is good." As in, don't spend thousands on a fancy microphone and gear if you can get professional quality sound out of a cheaper rig. The public doesn't need to know how the hot dog gets made, they just want to enjoy the end product.

We could say the same thing about self-publishing books, "**If a cover looks good, it is good.**" Similar to my voice-over rule, if a graphic designer from a developing country can deliver you an attractive eBook cover for $20, go ahead and try them. You can see samples of cover designers' work if you search on Fiverr. Some of my favorite cover designs for my own books didn't even cost up to $100. The cover of this book was only $20.

3. **Design your cover last.** You will want to get the cover for the eBook, audiobook, and print book all designed at the same time. These 3 covers are all slightly different-sized variations of the same design.

When getting the cover for the print edition made, you will need to know the number of pages the full manuscript contains—the size of the book spine is determined by the total number of pages in the book. Going back so the designer can adjust the print cover size when you are finally publishing your book is annoying. Just wait until you know how many pages will be in the final product before you execute this stage.

4. **Don't let text that hasn't been looked at by an editor ever reach the public.** By the time I finally publish a book, I have read and re-read my own words so many times while editing that I become blind to my own errors. I *always* use an editor. And not just an editor, if you can have several people read the unfinished work before you publish it, go ahead and do that. If you publish something and there turns out to be a glaring typo on the first page, you will be mortified. Don't ask me how I know this.

5. **Don't panic too much if you publish a typo.** You are a self-publisher, so it is easy enough to self-

correct. Just have the typo fixed and re-upload your files. The fixed content should be corrected on the consumer's end in just a couple of hours.

Once I published a book and when I visited the Kindle Store to verify things were kosher, it turned out I had published the cover with the graphic designer's watermark **STILL ON THE COVER OF MY BOOK.** The watermark was almost the same color as the book cover's background, so that's how I overlooked it. I had a number of pre-orders for this title, so I almost keeled over right there and then. However, I reached out to the designer, had the cover fixed, and re-uploaded the work overnight. All my readers woke up the next day and got their copy of the book with the fixed cover, and they were all unaware of the cover snafu (I hope).

6. **Go ahead and make an audiobook.** People are very attached to their format of choice. For example, certain readers will always prefer the paper pages and feel of a physical book. I am a

minimalist, so I hate clutter and usually only purchase eBooks. I read them on my phone or my iPad.

Finally, some people are completely devoted to audiobooks. I feel like many authors are still unaware of the power of audiobooks because audiobooks only became mainstream during the past decade.

I make more money from my audiobooks than eBooks and paperbacks combined. I realized why audiobooks dominate a certain section of the population while living in Los Angeles. People spend 10 – 20 hours in their cars commuting each week, so audiobook aficionados will listen to lots of audiobooks in their cars. Also, audiobooks don't make any clutter, so if you get the audiobook for *The Da Vinci Code*, you won't have it sitting in your house collecting dust for eons after you read it (like a paperback copy will). It will be up in the cloud with all your other audiobooks, ready to entertain you during that morning traffic.

This being said, you probably don't have the gear or the know-how to create your own audiobook yet. To assist with this are voice talents on ACX (Amazon's company that publishes audiobooks to Audible) that you can hire to deliver your audiobook masterpiece.

YOUR NOM DE PLUME

A lot of writers ask me if they need to use a pen name. As someone who has had their identity stolen, I think you should.

Out of the blue one day, the police called me at a day job in California to tell me someone had made a "reloadable credit card" with my name on it and was using it to check into motels in Broward County, Florida. To this day, the U.S. government seems to have a record of me living in Broward County—a place I have never been to—which is sort of ironic because I'm currently based just south of there in Miami. Use a pen name so "Florida Man" doesn't leave a trail of misinformation about you across the globe. Read on for my full take on using a pen name.

Once your book is out, strangers will have access to the name and information associated with your title. Depending on your specialty, maybe you don't want the receptionist at the dentist or that random dude you were trying to duck at a bar to know who you are. And though I want you to become a successful, self-published millionaire, the reality is you will probably still need a day job. Do you want your boss to know what you're writing? Do you want the boss of your boss to know what you're writing? Or that grouchy lady at HR you've been trying to avoid (she's such a pain)? Think long and hard about just who you want to share your writing with and how much you want them to know about you.

As a creative person, I feel freer when writing under a pen name. I caught myself holding back when trying to publish under my government name, Charles Ayres. I ended up regretting putting out my first book, *Impossibly Glamorous*, under my real name. I had wanted to use a pen name from the jump, but a couple of editors I was working with convinced me to use my real name. They argued that because it's a memoir, using my real name would lend more gravity to the work—they had a valid point.

Take into account the genre you are writing in as well. If you work at a university and are publishing a non-fiction book of your research, you might find it preferable to use your real name, since your professional reputation will get a boost from having a book out. If you are writing self-published erotica about lesbian vampires from outer space—but work at an investment bank—think about how Rochelle at your HR department might take it. Rochelle might be into lesbian vampire erotica, but there is a 99% chance she won't be.

I also wanted to use a pen name for a more sensible reason: my government name (Ayres) is not familiar to a lot of people. Most people cannot spell my surname correctly—and if they can—they cannot pronounce it ("Ayres" rhymes with "bears"). Is the name you want to publish under easy to spell? Will consumers Google you easily? Does your name roll off the tongue? I began using a pen name for much the same reasons Stephanie Germanotta is Lady Gaga. Maybe it's *not that hard* to spell, but it's a lot for the average consumer to remember. Also, I just wanted a name that sounded a bit more "fun." Sort of like how Caryn Elayne Johnson became Whoopi Goldberg or Eric Marlon Bishop became Jamie Foxx. Then again, I take a comedic angle in most of my work, so this works for my chosen genre.

Charles St. Anthony came into existence when I released my second book. *Impossibly Glamorous* came out in 2011, and it was well-received. I still had a day job, but I felt free to express my artistic side. A couple of years later, I was wrapping up my second book, *San Francisco Daddy*, and I caught myself holding back in my writing because of my real name. For comedy to work in today's world, you can't be bashful about dropping a couple of "F-bombs." Also, in *San Francisco Daddy*, I wanted to write a frank discourse around LGBTQ+ sexuality and dating. Not only that, but after a period of intermittent employment, I had gotten my first proper job in years—I didn't want to rock the boat. I didn't want Rochelle from HR to call me in one day and ask, "What's this you are writing about power bottoms and muscle bears?" Most jobs today will advertise an inclusive environment, but even if my boss was cool with it, like I said, what would the boss of my boss think? And I really didn't want Rochelle breathing down my neck about power bottoms.

So I decided to use a pen name for the second book and was thinking about what name to choose. I had been going to a program at a church in San Francisco … a program with steps. As in 12 Steps. It was at the Church of Saint Anthony, and I thought one day "Charles St. Anthony. That has a nice ring to it." And that was how Charles St. Anthony was born. I enjoy using a pen name as a kind of "drag"—not like a drag queen dressing as a woman. I mean drag as sort of a "persona for entertainment" that is detached from my private life. It's just how I compartmentalize "what I do" and "who I am." The only problem I have is that I have to fight for rankings in the Google search with the historical Saint Anthony of Padua. I know he is a Saint and all, so I hope he forgives me for writing about power bottoms. Or maybe Saint Anthony of Padua was a power bottom? His cloak and clerical staff look a bit twee. Highly suspect, wouldn't you agree?

THE 800-POUND GORILLA

A man named Michael Hart created the first eBook back in 1971—he used a mainframe computer to digitize the American Declaration of Independence. Several companies began selling eBooks in earnest as the digital age blossomed in the 1990s. It wasn't until the launch of the Amazon Kindle eBook reader in 2007 that the eBook format finally reached critical mass and become a media that the general public knew about and used.

As of 2020, the eBook market is estimated to record almost 200 million sales per year with sales reaching over $1 Billion. Print book sales still vastly outnumber eBooks, but 1 in 6 book sales in recent years are of eBooks.

With Amazon being such a key player in the eBook phenomenon, it isn't an enormous surprise that they are still the 800-Pound Gorilla in the room. Some authors only publish on Amazon via Kindle Unlimited and make all their money that way. Kindle eBook sales still dominate the market taking up 60 - 80% of all eBook sales. Amazon's dominance might leave a first-time author with many questions. For example, should you just publish via Amazon? Or should you "go wide" and upload to every eBook platform available? What's Sony Kobo? Should you care?

Ultimately, Amazon offers incentives in the form of marketing support and the ability to offer your work via a subscription service called "Kindle Unlimited." Kindle Unlimited subscription service allows readers to read as much content as they want of titles included in Kindle Unlimited.

To be in Kindle Unlimited, you will need to publish your book only on Amazon. Amazon has bots that search the Internet to make sure you are not publishing on another platform if you are part of Kindle Unlimited. You can't offer your work on Barnes & Noble Nook, Apple Books, and more. There are more than 1 billion iPhones out in the market where people could be reading your work.

Are you sure you don't want your book to be available to them as well?

I don't have all the answers. I don't even pretend to. From my personal experience, I can tell you that in some cases, you might want to keep your work exclusive to Amazon, and in other cases, you might go wide and publish on every platform available. You should not ignore Amazon, as they are the current leader in the eBook market by a large margin, and Amazon will continue to be the leader for years to come.

- To publish your eBook, first, you need to sign up on "Kindle Direct Publishing" (KDP). Go back to Chapter 2 if you haven't done this yet.

- In the KDP system, you can publish your print and eBook editions in one place. Audiobooks will be at ACX, but that is also owned by Amazon.

- Once you publish, you have the option of joining "Kindle Select" which gives you access to certain marketing options, and Kindle Unlimited. Subscribers of Kindle Unlimited can read as much content as they want of books that are part of the service.

- A book has to be exclusive to Amazon during the time it's available for Kindle Select. For example, you can make your book free for several days as a promotion if you put your work in Kindle Unlimited. It doesn't cost you any money to be part of Kindle Unlimited. It might be worth your while. As I mentioned before, there are authors who make their entire income by staying in Kindle Unlimited so readers can binge-read their entire series easily.

- Most authors that make use of Kindle Unlimited are authors of romance or other genres that lend themselves to binge-reading.

I release my books exclusively to Kindle for 3 - 6 months, then I publish them on other platforms. As mentioned earlier, I also use a platform called Draft2Digital to publish on Barnes & Noble, Apple, Kobo, and multiple other platforms at the same time. It is up to you whether you want to stay exclusive to Amazon forever. I don't like to put all my eggs in one basket, though, so I eventually make my books available on as many platforms as possible. Kindle (KDP) also allows you to publish your paperback. There is another service called Ingram Spark that offers slightly higher quality paperback printing, but Ingram Spark charges a book setup fee while KDP is free.

Pro Tip! When you are about to publish, be sure to use the eBook preview tool which is in the "Content" section of KDP when you are publishing your book. This is an absolute must for me because often in the file conversion of an eBook, there are foreign accent marks such as áçñü. Here you are trying to impress your readers by how cosmopolitan you are with your *umlauts* (ü) and your *tildes* (ñ), only to have Kindles and other eReaders mess it up by rendering the mark incorrectly. Sometimes the letter won't even appear at all.

Emojis will also be rendered incorrectly as well, so make sure to double-check them in the preview tool *before* you publish (😃 🫶 😈). Further, if you are making a print edition, have a print preview copy shipped to your house to check before you move your finger anywhere near the publish button. You will melt away and disappear like the Wicked Witch of the West in *The Wizard of Oz* if you publish a print edition and there is a glaring error right there in print for the world to see.

ODDS & ENDS

File Types:

- Once you have your manuscript finished, you will need to have your Doc file from Microsoft Word or Google Docs converted into an eBook file.

- Almost every platform these days takes a type of file called EPUB.

- For the paperback, you will need a special type of PDF. It is called a "print-ready PDF."

- When I put out my digital book, I'll place an order on Fiverr, and a programmer will deliver the epub and print-ready PDF all at once.

Advertising:

Unless you are already famous or have a large public platform, you will need to budget for online advertising. Amazon's ads are where I have had the most success in advertising. Think about it—people on Amazon are already thinking about buying something, so you need to help Amazon find your target readers through some savvy advertising. Amazon's advertising system is pretty complex, so I recommend looking at some online tutorials before trying them out.

- Each author has different experiences with online advertising. I believe the best way is to set up ads through your Amazon KDP account. These ads have brought me sales.

- Other authors have had a good experience with FaceBook ads, though they didn't really lead to sales in my experience.

- I don't advise putting out a self-published book without advertising. I suggest you experiment with different ads on Amazon once your book is out. It's within your KDP account and easy to set up yourself.

Audiobook:

- You can create an account on ACX (also owned by Amazon) and hire a voice actor directly on the platform.

- Recording and editing an audiobook takes a long time. In the end, you'll want them to deliver a sound file called an MP3. You will upload it to ACX and publish it. It should be available on Audible in a few weeks.

- ACX allows you to hire your voice-over artist via "flat rate" or "royalty share." As you might guess, in "royalty share," you split a percent of the royalties of the audiobook with the voice actor. I would stay away from this as most experienced voice-over artists know this isn't a good way to make money (until you are an established author with a massive following).

- I recommend offering the voice actor a flat rate. You can check out various voice actors on ACX.

Reach out to voice talent and get them to audition by submitting a short sample of your work (maybe a paragraph or 2).

- The audiobook must include an intro and an outro, and you'll have a "retail sample" between one and five minutes long.

- You will probably want to hire an expert for your audiobook. Many technical things can go wrong. If you are not an audio expert, you probably want to leave the audio editing to someone with experience. You can spend months on an audiobook, finally submit it to Audible, wait weeks for them to review it, and your audiobook might still get rejected on some technical issue that you don't have the skills to fix easily. To avoid this nightmare, just find a nice voice actor who knows the audiobook process well.

- Here are the technical requirements for ACX (Audible), and as you can see, it's quite a lot to take in:

https://www.acx.com/help/acx-audio-submission-re-quirements/201456300

LEGAL MATTERS

'll preface this by saying I am not an attorney, and you might need an attorney that specializes in publishing/arts before you publish anything. This is especially important if you are releasing a non-fiction book such as a memoir. There are possible legal issues regarding your work that you might not have even considered, and you need to protect your-self. **If you are writing a memoir or some kind of non-fiction, you have 2 choices:**

1. **Have anyone you are describing sign a release.**

2. **Change details about people mentioned in your work to the point where they become unrecog-nizable in your book.**

You want to get signed releases so you don't leave yourself at risk of a libel case. I'm sure you learned what libel was in school, but let's refresh your memory. *Merriam-Webster* defines "libel" as:

"A written or oral defamatory statement or representation that conveys an unjustly unfavorable representation."

So basically, talking shit about people. Libel is essentially the same as "slander"—but libel implies the written form of defamation. Libel is also notoriously difficult to prove in court—the plaintiff has to prove the defendant knowingly made a false statement that damaged someone's reputation. Not only that, a court will consider whether the statement was made "with actual malice." So were they purposely talking shit (false shit!) to fuck up your reputation? That's libel.

Whether or not libel is easy to prove, someone still might sue you just to mess with you. If you are going to be talking shit about someone in print (and getting famous as a result of said shit-talking), don't put it past the person you are talking shit about to drag you into court by your hair. If anything, they might get satisfaction by bleeding you dry with attorney's fees.

If you are writing about someone who is a private citizen and not a public figure while using the private citizen's actual name, it would be wise to get them to sign a release. If you are talking about a public figure, then you don't need to worry about this. Let's say you want to write about the day you ran into Beyoncé at Burger King. You don't need to call Parkwood in New York and ask Beyoncé to sign a release. An attorney will probably tell you it's in your best interest to get absolutely everyone to sign a release, but Beyoncé is planning a world tour and doesn't have time to chat with you. Knowledge about a famous person is of general interest to the public, so as long as you are not defaming a famous person by lying and writing something that will hurt their reputation, you should be in the clear.

A famous person's attorneys might still send you a "cease and desist" if they don't like what you've written. The conventional wisdom in Hollywood has been that discussing a famous person's alleged drug use or sexuality is a couple of ways to get a cease and desist pretty quickly. If you claim you saw a famous person doing hard drugs such as cocaine or heroin, then a TV or movie production might not insure them. If the actor can't get insured then they lose their income, and guess what? That defamation lawsuit might be coming your way.

If what you are claiming is true and not written with actual malice, then you should be on the right side of the law. And let's get real. Famous people and their legal teams are generally more concerned with what *Page 6* or *The Daily Mail* might say about them than about a small independent author. It's up to you what kind of risks you are willing to take when you are writing.

Returning the discussion to people who aren't public figures, if you are still in touch with the person you are writing about, you should ask them to sign a release as well. You need to protect yourself not just from libel issues, but things like violating a person's privacy. Also, making ethical choices will benefit you in the long run. If someone was writing about you, wouldn't you want them to give you a heads-up before their book came out.?

If you don't wish to contact someone from your past, you would probably want to change their name, places, and other details so they can't come after you. In my writing, I've gone so far as to change someone's gender, ethnicity, and nationality so they will be utterly unrecognizable. As long as the overall tone of your book doesn't change, it's an easy way to protect yourself. Another option is to make someone a "composite character" of several people you have known. A composite character is so you can claim in court that the character you are referring to in your book is not just a solitary person, but a Frankenstein's monster of bits and pieces of various people you have met! I'm unsure how well the "composite character" gambit works in court, but it is another tool to have under your belt in case you find yourself defending your writing from litigation.

If all of this sounds too daunting, you might consider changing your work to a fiction or a novel that is merely informed by your past experiences. It is a tough decision. You want your story out there. Your story is valid. You want recognition for all you have overcome and achieved. But make sure you put out your work in a way that will lead to greater success for you and avoid legal entanglements that will drag you down. When you have an attorney draw up release forms, also see if he'll give you a good disclaimer to put in your book if you need one.

Once your book is out, you might wonder if you need to register the copyright. The minute you write a sentence on a page, you already own the copyright. Registering the copyright will simply bolster your legal case should you need to engage in litigation to protect your work. Again, this is up to you. How much money are you willing to invest in this self-publishing project? I say if you have the funds for it, go ahead and register your work with the Copyright Office in your country. It's another layer of protection that you can show an attorney, a judge, or even Amazon that you are the true owner of a written work.

GET WRITING!

Dear Aspiring Author,

You now have the knowledge you need to write your great masterpiece. With great knowledge comes great power. Remember your story is important and valid. Don't let anybody put you down for being self-published.

If you think about it, most of the Classics of Antiquity were self-published. Homer, Socrates, and Plato all wrote things down, and we remember them today because of their quality. It's not like Simon & Schuster had a branch office in ancient Athens. These men wrote things of lasting value, and truly great art has a way of rising to the top no matter how it is put out.

Now comes the time for a little discipline. Surely you've met someone that goes around saying they are writing a book. Don't be one of them. In my experience, the people that write a book are the ones that don't run around telling people that's what they are doing. Just like that person from your office that goes around telling people about their latest diet, and you catch them stuffing their faces with donuts three days later, the "I'm writing a book" people are very rarely the ones who get published. They get an ego boost and attention from talking about writing a book, whereas I want you to have the satisfaction of actually having something out.

Don't overwhelm yourself, but see if you can start by writing one page per day. Set aside a certain time and a certain space to focus on your writing and just write one page. If you write one page a day for three or four months, you should have your book. Now get out there and get to writing!

If you found this book entertaining and educational, I implore you to take a look at my other books: *Impossibly Glamorous*, *San Francisco Daddy*, *Uber Diva*, *DTLA Hustler*, *Beverly Hills Postmate*, and *Saints & Sinners in Oklahoma City*.

Also, please consider leaving a review at your favorite online retailer. Thank you for reading. Find me on social media @kingcharles0921. May your days be filled with joy and abundance! *Bonne chance, mes amies!*

 -Charles St. Anthony

GLOSSARY OF TERMS

ACX - Platform where authors, voice actors, and publishers come together to create audiobooks. Audiobooks through ACX are released on Audible, a company owned by Amazon.

Barnes & Noble Nook - eBook reader created by bookstore chain Barnes & Noble.

EPUB (Electronic Publication) file - File that once converted from a .doc or .docx file will be readable on eBook readers.

Fiverr - Platform where freelance writers, designers, programmers, and artists from across the world offer their services.

HTML (HyperText Markup) - Coding language for documents to be viewed in a web browser. eBook files are usually .doc files converted to HTML.

Ingram Spark - Print-on-demand platform.

ISBN (International Standard Book Number) - A unique number and identifier that is associated with a book.

KDP (Kindle Direct Publishing) - Self-publishing platform that allows users to release eBooks on Kindle as well as paperback books.

Kindle E-reader - Tablet device via Amazon that allows people to read eBooks.

Kindle Select - A KDP program that authors can enroll in so that their book is available to readers in the Kindle Unlimited subscription service.

Kindle Unlimited - Amazon subscription service that allows readers to read as much as they want from Amazon's eBook library and is a part of the Unlimited program.

Libel - Defamation of a person's character in print.

MOBI file - Type of eBook file that was created by Mobipocket. Mobipocket was purchased by Amazon, and the MOBI file was the original eBook format that Kindle eBooks were created from.

MP3 (MPEG1 Audio Layer III) – Digital audio file used in music, spoken word, and audiobooks.

Print-ready PDF – PDF file that arranges a book for the print edition.

Slander – Verbally defaming someone's character.

Sony Kobo - eBook reader released by Sony corporation.

Udemy – Platform for online teaching and learning.

Upwork – Platform where freelance writers, designers, programmers, and artists from across the world offer their services.

ACKNOWLEDGEMENTS

Thank you to all my friends over at the hostel in South Beach that I stayed while writing this work. You have my gratitude. May you be blessed with joy and abundance.

Also, thank you to everyone who contributed to my GoFundMe "Miami Book Project." I will give a thank you in that book to everyone who donated. Contribute here:

https://www.gofundme.com/f/miami-book-project

I give a heartfelt thank you to the following as well as several anonymous donors:

William Ayres

Cydonie Fukami

Marcella Hammer

Lorna Handa

Christine Kawaguchi

Todd Phillips

Elizabeth Shoemaker

Emmie Smith

And of course I always thank Judy Itoh for the encouragement.

The Miami Book Project is a work-in-progress, so I appreciate everyone's support.

I need your support to keep making my educational and entertaining content. Please donate to my GoFundMe. If you just want to give me a tip and buy me a latté find @kingcharles0921 on Venmo or Cashapp.

ABOUT THE AUTHOR

Charles Ayres, a native of Kansas City, publishes under the pen name Charles St. Anthony. A graduate of Columbia University in New York City. He has published two humorous memoirs and a series of humorous short reads on the gig economy. His podcast *T with Charles* features interviews with various entertainers, artists, and personalities from around the globe. Find Charles on social media under the handle @kingcharles0921.

Charles also works as a publishing coach, helping aspiring writers get published. Got a book you are looking to publish traditionally? Reach out to Charles at https://publishingcoachcharles.com/home/.

DISCLAIMERS

The thoughts and opinions expressed here are entirely the author's own and do not represent the thoughts and views of Amazon, Barnes & Noble, Microsoft, Google, Sony, or any other entity mentioned herein.

This publication may contain copyrighted material. Under section 107 of the Copyright Act 1976, allowance is made for "fair use" for purposes such as criticism, comment, news reporting, teaching, scholarship, education, and research.

The thoughts and opinions provided by I.G. Studios LLC in *Charles' Quick Guide to Self-Publishing* are for general informational purposes only. All the work in the publication is provided in good faith, however, we make no representation or warranty of any kind, express or implied, regarding the accuracy, adequacy, validity, reliability, availability, or completeness of any information in this publication. UNDER NO CIRCUM-STANCE WILL WE HAVE ANY LIABILITY TO YOU FOR ANY LOSS OR DAMAGE OF ANY KIND INCURRED AS A RESULT OF THE USE OF THE PUBLICATION OR RELI-ANCE ON ANY INFORMATION CONTAINED HEREIN. YOUR USE OF THE SITE AND RELIANCE ON ANY IN-FORMATION ON THE SITE IS SOLELY AT YOUR OWN RISK.

This publication contains links to third-party websites or content belonging to or originating from third parties. WE DO NOT WARRANT, ENDORSE, GUARANTEE, OR ASSUME RESPONSIBILITY FOR ANY INFORMATION OFFERED BY THIRD-PARTY WEBSITES. WE WILL NOT BE RESPONSIBLE FOR MONITORING ANY INTERAC-TION BETWEEN YOU AND THIRD-PARTY WEBSITES.

The publishing information is provided for educational or informational purposes only and is not a substitute for professional advice. Accordingly, before taking any actions based on the information contained herein, we encourage you to consult with the appropriate profes-sionals.

REFERENCES

"16 Celebrities Shared the Reason They Picked a Stage Name, And (sic) Some of These Surprised Me." *Buzzfeed*. Retrieved 1 December 2022.

"Disclaimer." *Termly*. Retrieved 8 Nov. 2022.

"How Do You Prove a Defamation of Character Claim." *The Law Dictionary*. Retrieved 8 Nov. 2022.

"Libel." *Merriam-Webster.com Dictionary*, Retrieved 8 Nov. 2022.

Smith, Olivia. "A Brief History of eBooks." Bookscouter. 27 June, 2022. Retrieved 2 November 2022.

Watson, Amy. "E-books in the U.S. - Statistics and Facts" Statista. 3 December 2021. Retrieved 2 November 2022.

"With More Bookstores Open, Soaring E-books (Sic) Sales Fall Back to Earth." NPD. 6 October 2021. Retrieved 2 November 2022.

Fin.

www.ingramcontent.com/pod-product-compliance
Lightning Source LLC
Chambersburg PA
CBHW041652150726

48005CB00013BA/1675